Light Cooking™

ITALIAN

Healthy, Low Fat and Delicious!

PUBLICATIONS INTERNATIONAL, LTD.

Food Guide Pyramid source: U.S. Department of Agriculture/U.S. Department of Health and Human Services.

Recipe Development: Roberta L. Duyff, M.S., R.D., C.H.E.
Nutritional Analysis: Linda R. Yoakam, M.S., R.D.

Photography: Photo/Kevin Smith, Chicago
Photographers: Kevin Smith, Doug Hunter
Prop Stylist: Lucianne Crowley
Food Stylists: Tobe LeMoine, Irene Bertolucci, Diane Hugh
Assistant Food Stylist: Megan North
Photo Assistant: Greg Shapps

Pictured on the front cover: Fusilli Pizzaiola with Turkey Meatballs *(page 50)*.
Pictured on the inside front cover: Fresh Vegetable Lasagna *(page 42)*.
Pictured on the inside back cover: Roasted Pepper Pizza *(page 54)*.
Pictured on the back cover *(from top to bottom):* Mushroom-Clam Sauce *(page 76)*, Hearty Minestrone *(page 20)*, Pepper-Stuffed Artichokes *(page 60)* and Polenta Apricot Pudding Cake *(page 86)*.

ISBN: 0-7853-1185-8

Manufactured in U.S.A.

8 7 6 5 4 3 2 1

Microwave Cooking: Microwave ovens vary in wattage. The microwave cooking times given in this publication are approximate. Use the cooking times as guidelines and check for doneness before adding more time. Consult manufacturer's instructions for suitable microwave-safe cooking dishes.

CONTENTS

LESSONS IN SMART EATING

Today, people everywhere are more aware than ever before about the importance of maintaining a healthful lifestyle. In addition to proper exercise, this includes eating foods that are lower in fat, sodium and cholesterol. The goal of *Light Cooking* is to provide today's cook with easy-to-prepare recipes that taste great, yet easily fit into your dietary goals. Eating well is a matter of making smarter choices about the foods you eat. Preparing the recipes in *Light Cooking* is your first step toward making smart choices a delicious reality.

A Balanced Diet

The U.S. Department of Agriculture and the Department of Health and Human Services have developed a Food Guide Pyramid to illustrate how easy it is to eat a healthier diet. It is not a rigid prescription, but rather a general guide that lets you choose a healthful diet that's right for you. It calls for eating a wide variety of foods to get the nutrients you need and, at the same time, the right amount of calories to maintain a healthy weight.

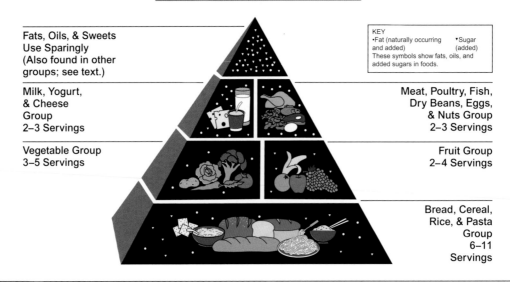

Food Guide Pyramid
A Guide to Daily Food Choices

Fats, Oils, & Sweets
Use Sparingly
(Also found in other groups; see text.)

KEY
•Fat (naturally occurring and added)   ▼Sugar (added)
These symbols show fats, oils, and added sugars in foods.

Milk, Yogurt, & Cheese Group
2–3 Servings

Meat, Poultry, Fish, Dry Beans, Eggs, & Nuts Group
2–3 Servings

Vegetable Group
3–5 Servings

Fruit Group
2–4 Servings

Bread, Cereal, Rice, & Pasta Group
6–11 Servings

The number of servings, and consequently, the number of calories a person can eat each day, is determined by a number of factors, including age, weight, height, activity level and gender. Sedentary women and some older adults need about 1,600 calories each day. For most children, teenage girls, active women and many sedentary men 2,000 calories is about right. Teenage boys, active men and some very active women use about 2,800 calories each day. Use the chart below to determine how many servings you need for your calorie level.

Personalized Food Group Servings for Different Calorie Levels*			
	1,600	2,000	2,800
Bread Group Servings	6	8	11
Vegetable Group Servings	3	4	5
Fruit Group Servings	2	3	4
Milk Group Servings	2–3**	2–3**	2–3**
Meat Group Servings (ounces)	5	6	7

* Numbers may be rounded.
** Women who are pregnant or breast-feeding, teenagers and young adults to age 24 need 3 or more servings.

Lower Fat for Healthier Living

It is widely known that most Americans' diets are too high in fat. A low fat diet reduces your risk of getting certain diseases and helps you maintain a healthy weight. Studies have shown that eating more than the recommended amount of fat (especially saturated fat) is associated with increased blood cholesterol levels in some adults. A high blood cholesterol level is associated with increased risk for heart disease. A high fat diet may also increase your chances for obesity and some types of cancer.

Nutrition experts recommend diets that contain 30% or less of total daily calories from fat. The "30% calories from fat" goal applies to a total diet over time, not to a single food, serving of a recipe or meal. To find the approximate percentage of calories from fat use this easy 3-step process:

1 Multiply the grams of fat per serving by 9 (there are 9 calories in each gram of fat), to give you the number of calories from fat per serving.

2 Divide by the total number of calories per serving.

3 Multiply by 100%.

For example, imagine a 200 calorie sandwich that has 10 grams of fat.
To find the percentage of calories from fat, first multiply the grams of fat by 9:
$$10 \times 9 = 90$$

Then, divide by the total number of calories in a serving:
$$90 \div 200 = .45$$

Multiply by 100% to get the percentage of calories from fat:
$$.45 \times 100\% = 45\%$$

You may find doing all this math tiresome, so an easier way to keep track of the fat in your diet is to calculate the total *grams* of fat appropriate to your caloric intake, then keep a running count of fat grams over the course of a day. The Nutrition Reference Chart on page 92 lists recommended daily fat intakes based on calorie level.

Defining "Fat Free"

It is important to take the time to read food labels carefully. For example, you'll find many food products on the grocery store shelves making claims such as "97% fat free." This does not necessarily mean that 97% of the *calories* are free from fat (or that only 3 percent of calories come from fat). Often these numbers are calculated by weight. This means that out of 100 grams of this food, 3 grams are fat. Depending on what else is in the food, the percentage of calories from fat can be quite high. You may find that the percent of calories *from fat* can be as high as 50%.

Daily Values

Fat has become the focus of many diets and eating plans. This is because most Americans' diets are too high in fat. However, there are other important nutrients to be aware of, including saturated fat, sodium, cholesterol, protein, carbohydrates and several vitamins and minerals. Daily values for these nutrients have been established by the government and reflect current nutritional recommendations for a 2,000 calorie reference diet. They are appropriate for most adults and children (age 4 or older) and provide excellent guidelines for an overall healthy diet. The chart on page 92 gives the daily values for 11 different items.

Nutritional Analysis

Every recipe in *Light Cooking* is followed by a nutritional analysis block that lists certain nutrient values for a single serving.

■ The analysis of each recipe includes all the ingredients that are listed in that recipe, *except* ingredients labeled as "optional" or "for garnish."

■ If a range is given in the yield of a recipe ("Makes 6 to 8 servings" for example), the *lower* yield was used to calculate the per serving information.

■ If a range is offered for an ingredient ("¼ to ⅛ teaspoon" for example), the *first* amount given was used to calculate the nutrition information.

■ If an ingredient is presented with an option ("2 cups hot cooked rice or noodles" for example), the *first* item listed was used to calculate the nutritional information.

■ Foods shown in photographs on the same serving plate and offered as "serve with" suggestions at the end of a recipe are *not* included in the recipe analysis unless they are listed in the ingredient list.

■ Meat should be trimmed of all visible fat since this is reflected in the nutritional analysis.

■ In recipes calling for cooked rice or noodles, the analysis was based on rice or noodles that were prepared without added salt or fat unless otherwise mentioned in the recipe.

The nutrition information that appears with each recipe was calculated by an independent nutrition consulting firm. Every effort has been made to check the accuracy of these numbers. However, because numerous variables account for a wide range of values in certain foods, all analyses that appear in this book should be considered approximate.

The recipes in this publication are *not* intended as a medically therapeutic program, nor as a substitute for medically approved diet plans for people on fat, cholesterol or sodium restricted diets. You should consult your physician before beginning any diet plan. The recipes offered here can be a part of a healthy lifestyle that meets recognized dietary guidelines. A healthy lifestyle includes not only eating a balanced diet, but engaging in proper exercise as well.

All the ingredients called for in these recipes are generally available in large supermarkets, so there is no need to go to specialty or health food stores. You'll also see an ever-increasing amount of reduced fat and nonfat products available in local markets. Take advantage of these items to reduce your daily fat intake even more.

Cooking Healthier

When cooking great-tasting low fat meals, you will find some techniques or ingredients are different from traditional cooking. Fat serves as a flavor enhancer and gives foods a distinctive and desirable texture. In order to compensate for the lack of fat and still give great-tasting results, many of the *Light Cooking* recipes call for a selection of herbs or a combination of fresh vegetables. A wide variety of grains and pastas are also used. Many of the recipes call for alternative protein sources, such as dried beans or tofu. Often meat is included in a recipe as an accent flavor rather than the star attraction. Vegetables are often "sautéed" in a small amount of broth rather than oil. Applesauce may be added to baked goods to give a texture similar to full fat foods. These are all simple changes that you can easily make when you start cooking healthy!

Italian Ingredients

Great Italian food starts with fresh, authentic ingredients. These ingredients can be found in most supermarkets and Italian groceries.

Arborio Rice: This Italian-grown, short-grain rice has large, plump grains with a distinctively nutty taste. Arborio rice is traditionally used for risotto dishes because its high starch content allows it to absorb more liquid than regular or long-grain rice, thus producing a creamy texture.

Cannellini Beans: These large, white Italian kidney beans are available both in dried and canned forms. Dried beans need to be soaked in water several hours or overnight to rehydrate before cooking; canned beans should be rinsed and drained to freshen the beans. Great Northern beans make a good substitute.

Capers: A bush native to the Mediterranean produces these flower buds that are sun-dried, then pickled in a vinegar brine. Capers should be rinsed and drained before using to remove any excess salt.

Fennel: This is an anise-flavored, bulb-shaped vegetable with celerylike stems and feathery leaves. Purchase clean, crisp bulbs with no sign of browning; the greenery should be a fresh bright color. Store in the refrigerator, tightly wrapped in plastic, for up to five days.

Italian Plum Tomatoes: These are flavorful egg-shaped tomatoes that come in red and yellow varieties. As with other tomatoes, they are very perishable. Choose firm tomatoes that are fragrant and free of blemishes. Ripe tomatoes should be stored at room temperature and used within a few days. Canned tomatoes are a good substitute when fresh ones are out of season.

Parmesan Cheese: This is a hard, dry cheese that is made from skimmed cow's milk. This cheese has a straw-colored interior with a rich, sharp flavor. Parmesan cheese is primarily used grated. While pregrated cheese is available, it doesn't compare with freshly grated. Pieces of Parmesan can be stored in the refrigerator, loosely wrapped in plastic, for a few weeks. Refrigerate freshly grated Parmesan in an airtight container for up to one week or freeze for up to three months.

Ricotta Cheese: This white, moist cheese has a slightly sweet flavor, is rich, fresh and slightly grainy, but is smoother than cottage cheese. Ricotta cheese can be found in regular, low fat and nonfat varieties. It is often used in lasagna and manicotti dishes. When purchasing cheese, check the expiration date; store tightly covered in the refrigerator.

Sun-Dried Tomatoes: The drying of fresh, ripe tomatoes in the sun results in chewy, intensely flavored, sweet tomatoes called sun-dried tomatoes. These tomatoes add rich flavor to sauces, soups, salads and many other dishes. To rehydrate sun-dried tomatoes, simply pour 1 cup boiling water over tomatoes in a small heatproof bowl. Let tomatoes soak for 5 to 10 minutes or until they become soft, then drain.

HEALTHY BEGINNINGS

SWEET PEPPER GARLIC SOUP

Eating garlic may help to dissolve blood clots that could trigger heart attacks and strokes.

2 teaspoons olive oil
½ cup chopped onion
6 cloves garlic, chopped
1 cup cubed potato, unpeeled
1 cup chopped red bell peppers
3½ cups ⅓-less-salt chicken broth
1 cup low fat cottage cheese
2 tablespoons plain nonfat yogurt
⅛ teaspoon ground black pepper

1 Heat oil in medium saucepan over medium heat; add onion and garlic. Cook and stir 3 minutes or until onion is tender. Add potato, bell peppers and broth. Bring to a boil; reduce heat and simmer 10 to 15 minutes or until potato is easily pierced when tested with fork. Remove from heat; cool completely.

2 Place broth mixture in food processor or blender; process until smooth. Refrigerate until completely cool.

3 Place cottage cheese and yogurt in food processor or blender; process until smooth. Set aside ¼ cup cheese mixture. Stir remaining cheese mixture into chilled broth mixture until well blended. Add black pepper; stir well. Top with reserved cheese mixture. Garnish with parsley and bell pepper strips, if desired.

Makes 6 (¾-cup) servings

Nutrients per Serving:

Calories	105
(19% of calories from fat)	
Total Fat	2 g
Saturated Fat	0 g
Cholesterol	2 mg
Sodium	180 mg
Carbohydrate	15 g
Dietary Fiber	2 g
Protein	7 g
Calcium	52 mg
Iron	1 mg
Vitamin A	28 RE
Vitamin C	40 mg

DIETARY EXCHANGES:
½ Starch/Bread, 1 Lean Meat, 1 Vegetable

WHITE BEAN AND ESCAROLE SOUP

Escarole has wide, slightly curved, pale green leaves with a mild flavor. Escarole has been used mainly in salads, but is wonderful cooked and used as a vegetable in soups and stews.

1½ cups dried baby lima beans
3 cups water
1 teaspoon olive oil
½ cup chopped celery
⅓ cup coarsely chopped onion
2 cloves garlic, minced
2 cans (10 ounces each) no-salt-added whole tomatoes, undrained, chopped
½ cup chopped fresh parsley
2 tablespoons fresh rosemary
¼ teaspoon ground black pepper
3 cups shredded fresh escarole

1 Place dried lima beans in large glass bowl; cover completely with water. Soak 6 to 8 hours or overnight. Drain beans; place in large saucepan or Dutch oven. Cover beans with 3 cups water; bring to a boil over high heat. Reduce heat to low. Cover and simmer about 1 hour or until soft. Drain; set aside.

2 Heat oil in small skillet over medium heat. Add celery, onion and garlic; cook until onion is tender. Remove from heat.

3 Add celery mixture and tomatoes with liquid to beans. Stir in parsley, rosemary and black pepper. Cover and simmer over low heat 15 minutes. Add escarole; simmer 5 minutes.
Makes 6 (1½-cup) servings

Nutrients per Serving:

Calories	196
(7% of calories from fat)	
Total Fat	2 g
Saturated Fat	0 g
Cholesterol	0 mg
Sodium	33 mg
Carbohydrate	35 g
Dietary Fiber	5 g
Protein	12 g
Calcium	80 mg
Iron	5 mg
Vitamin A	136 RE
Vitamin C	25 mg

DIETARY EXCHANGES:
2 Starch/Bread,
2 Vegetable

Cook's Tip

Fresh escarole is available throughout the year. However, it's at its best in the winter. Keep escarole refrigerated in a resealable plastic food storage bag for up to three days. Wash well, trim core end and tear by hand into small pieces.

FRESH TOMATO PASTA SOUP

*Tomatoes are one of our most
significant dietary sources
of vitamin C and
beta-carotene.*

Nutrients per Serving:

Calories	116
(28% of calories from fat)	
Total Fat	4 g
Saturated Fat	1 g
Cholesterol	4 mg
Sodium	62 mg
Carbohydrate	17 g
Dietary Fiber	2 g
Protein	5 g
Calcium	74 mg
Iron	2 mg
Vitamin A	122 RE
Vitamin C	34 mg

DIETARY EXCHANGES:
½ Starch/Bread,
2 Vegetable, ½ Fat

1 tablespoon olive oil
½ cup chopped onion
1 clove garlic, minced
3 pounds fresh tomatoes, coarsely chopped
3 cups ⅓-less-salt chicken broth
1 tablespoon minced fresh basil
1 tablespoon minced fresh marjoram
1 tablespoon minced fresh oregano
1 teaspoon fennel seed
½ teaspoon ground black pepper
¾ cup uncooked rosamarina or other small pasta
½ cup (2 ounces) shredded part-skim mozzarella cheese

1 Heat oil in large saucepan over medium heat. Add onion and garlic; cook and stir until onion is tender. Add tomatoes, broth, basil, marjoram, oregano, fennel seed and black pepper.

2 Bring to a boil; reduce heat. Cover; simmer 25 minutes. Remove from heat; cool slightly.

3 Purée tomato mixture in food processor or blender in batches. Return to saucepan; bring to a boil. Add pasta; cook 7 to 9 minutes or until tender. Transfer to serving bowls. Sprinkle with mozzarella. Garnish with marjoram sprigs, if desired.

Makes 8 (¾-cup) servings

Cook's Tip

Fresh basil will last three or four days if wrapped first in damp
towels, then in plastic wrap, and refrigerated. Wash basil leaves
and dry thoroughly. Leaves cut with a knife discolor quickly
and should only be used in cooked dishes.

ROMAN SPINACH SOUP

Traditionally called stracciatella, this classic Roman egg soup is made with spinach, which is high in beta-carotene, a form of vitamin A. Studies suggest that beta-carotene helps lower the risk of cancer and angina.

6 cups ⅓-less-salt chicken broth
1 cup cholesterol free egg substitute
¼ cup minced fresh basil
3 tablespoons freshly grated Parmesan cheese
2 tablespoons lemon juice
1 tablespoon minced fresh parsley
¼ teaspoon ground white pepper
⅛ teaspoon ground nutmeg
8 cups fresh spinach, washed, stems removed, chopped

1 Bring broth to a boil in 4-quart saucepan over medium heat.

2 Beat together egg substitute, basil, Parmesan, lemon juice, parsley, white pepper and nutmeg in small bowl. Set aside.

3 Stir spinach into broth; simmer 1 minute. Slowly pour egg mixture into broth mixture, whisking constantly so egg threads form. Simmer 2 to 3 minutes or until egg is cooked. Garnish with lemon slices, if desired. Serve immediately.

Makes 8 (¾-cup) servings

Note: Soup may look curdled.

Nutrients per Serving:

Calories	46
(22% of calories from fat)	
Total Fat	1 g
Saturated Fat	0 g
Cholesterol	2 mg
Sodium	153 mg
Carbohydrate	4 g
Dietary Fiber	1 g
Protein	6 g
Calcium	106 mg
Iron	2 mg
Vitamin A	538 RE
Vitamin C	18 mg

DIETARY EXCHANGES:
½ Lean Meat, ½ Vegetable

Cook's Tip
Do not store fresh spinach with apples, pears or tomatoes because these fruits give off a natural gas that can cause browning of the leaves.

HEARTY MINESTRONE

Italian for "big soup," minestrone refers to a thick vegetable soup that generally contains pasta and beans and is topped with grated Parmesan cheese and fresh parsley. This incredible soup is hearty enough to be a meal.

Nutrients per Serving:

Calories	191
(11% of calories from fat)	
Total Fat	2 g
Saturated Fat	1 g
Cholesterol	2 mg
Sodium	86 mg
Carbohydrate	35 g
Dietary Fiber	4 g
Protein	9 g
Calcium	116 mg
Iron	3 mg
Vitamin A	464 RE
Vitamin C	36 mg

DIETARY EXCHANGES:
1½ Starch/Bread,
2 Vegetable, ½ Fat

1 cup dried pinto beans
2 teaspoons olive oil
½ cup chopped red onion
1 clove garlic, minced
3 cans (10 ounces each) no-salt-added whole tomatoes, undrained, chopped
1 medium potato, cut into ½-inch cubes
1 cup coarsely chopped carrots
1 cup thinly sliced zucchini
4 ounces coarsely shredded cabbage
⅔ cup coarsely chopped leek
½ cup coarsely chopped celery
2 cups no-salt-added vegetable juice cocktail
2 cups water
1 tablespoon chopped fresh basil
1 teaspoon chopped fresh sage
2 bay leaves
¼ teaspoon ground black pepper
1 cup small shell pasta
4 tablespoons freshly grated Parmesan cheese
1 tablespoon chopped fresh parsley

1 Place dried pinto beans in large glass bowl; cover completely with water. Soak 6 to 8 hours or overnight. Drain beans; discard water.

2 Heat oil in large heavy saucepan or Dutch oven over medium heat. Add onion and garlic; cook and stir until onion is tender.

3 Drain tomatoes, reserving liquid. Add tomatoes to saucepan; mix well. Add pinto beans, potato, carrots, zucchini, cabbage, leek and celery. Stir in vegetable juice, water and reserved tomato liquid. Add basil, sage, bay leaves and black pepper. Bring to a boil over high heat; reduce heat. Cover and simmer 2 hours, stirring occasionally.

4 Add pasta to saucepan 15 minutes before serving. Cook, uncovered, until soup thickens. Remove bay leaves; discard. Top with Parmesan and parsley.

Makes 10 (1½-cup) servings

THREE-PEPPER TUNA SALAD

This incredible salad is simply bursting with nutrition! It contains low fat, high protein tuna, three kinds of vitamin-rich bell peppers, zucchini and tomatoes, all tossed in a wonderful olive oil and wine vinegar dressing.

2	cups thinly sliced zucchini
½	cup red bell pepper strips
½	cup green bell pepper strips
½	cup yellow bell pepper strips
1	cup cherry tomatoes, halved
1	can (6 ounces) solid albacore tuna packed in water, drained
¼	cup chopped green onions with tops
¼	cup chopped fresh basil
2½	tablespoons red wine vinegar
1	tablespoon olive oil
½	teaspoon minced fresh garlic
½	teaspoon fresh marjoram
⅛	teaspoon ground black pepper

 Pour ¾ cup water into medium saucepan. Add zucchini and bell pepper strips. Steam vegetables about 10 minutes or until crisp-tender. Remove from heat; drain any excess water. Transfer to large serving bowl. Add tomatoes, tuna, green onions and basil.

 Combine vinegar, oil, garlic, marjoram and black pepper in jar or bottle with tight-fitting lid; shake well. Pour dressing over vegetable mixture; mix well. Garnish as desired.

Makes 4 servings

Nutrients per Serving:

Calories	134
(31% of calories from fat)	
Total Fat	5 g
Saturated Fat	1 g
Cholesterol	18 mg
Sodium	175 mg
Carbohydrate	11 g
Dietary Fiber	3 g
Protein	14 g
Calcium	30 mg
Iron	1 mg
Vitamin A	145 RE
Vitamin C	94 mg

DIETARY EXCHANGES:
1½ Lean Meat,
2 Vegetable

❖

Cook's Tip

Fresh zucchini is available year-round. Select fairly small zucchini with blemish-free skin.

❖

BEAN & MUSHROOM SALAD WITH FRESH HERB DRESSING

Studies show that eating a half cup of cooked beans daily may reduce cholesterol levels as much as ten percent. Cooked beans also help regulate blood sugar levels, are high in fiber and linked to preventing certain types of cancers.

Nutrients per Serving:

Calories	111
(24% of calories from fat)	
Total Fat	3 g
Saturated Fat	0 g
Cholesterol	0 mg
Sodium	273 mg
Carbohydrate	17 g
Dietary Fiber	5 g
Protein	5 g
Calcium	35 mg
Iron	2 mg
Vitamin A	47 RE
Vitamin C	30 mg

DIETARY EXCHANGES:
1 Starch/Bread,
½ Vegetable, ½ Fat

1 can (16 ounces) red kidney beans, rinsed and drained
1 can (16 ounces) lima beans, rinsed and drained
1 cup sliced mushrooms
1 cup chopped green bell pepper
¼ cup chopped green onions with tops
   Fresh Herb Dressing (recipe follows)
1 cup cherry tomatoes, halved
10 leaves romaine lettuce (optional)

1 Combine kidney beans, lima beans, mushrooms, bell pepper and onions in large bowl. Prepare Fresh Herb Dressing. Add dressing to vegetable mixture. Cover; refrigerate 2 to 3 hours or overnight.

2 Add tomatoes to bean mixture; mix well. Serve on lettuce-lined plates, if desired. Garnish as desired.   *Makes 10 servings*

FRESH HERB DRESSING

½ cup red wine vinegar
2 tablespoons olive oil
1 clove garlic, crushed
1 tablespoon chopped fresh oregano
1 tablespoon chopped fresh marjoram
½ teaspoon sugar
⅛ teaspoon ground black pepper

1 Combine vinegar, oil, garlic, oregano, marjoram, sugar and black pepper in small bowl; mix well.   *Makes about ⅔ cup dressing*

SALAD PRIMAVERA

Primavera in Italian means "spring style." This fabulous salad combines nutritious greens, artichokes, bell peppers and oranges to create a unique "spring" dish.

Nutrients per Serving:

Calories	55
(14% of calories from fat)	
Total Fat	1 g
Saturated Fat	0 g
Cholesterol	1 mg
Sodium	102 mg
Carbohydrate	10 g
Dietary Fiber	3 g
Protein	3 g
Calcium	70 mg
Iron	1 mg
Vitamin A	170 RE
Vitamin C	44 mg

DIETARY EXCHANGES:
2 Vegetable

6 cups romaine lettuce, washed, torn into bite-sized pieces
1 package (9 ounces) frozen artichoke hearts, thawed, drained, cut into bite-sized pieces
1 cup chopped watercress
1 orange, peeled, separated into segments, cut into halves
½ cup chopped red bell pepper
¼ cup chopped green onions with tops
   Citrus-Caper Dressing (recipe follows)
2 tablespoons freshly grated Parmesan cheese

1 Combine lettuce, artichoke hearts, watercress, orange segments, bell pepper and green onions in large bowl. Prepare Citrus-Caper Dressing. Add dressing to lettuce mixture. Mix well. Sprinkle with Parmesan before serving.   *Makes 8 servings*

CITRUS–CAPER DRESSING

⅓ cup orange juice
¼ cup white wine vinegar
2 tablespoons chopped fresh parsley
2 teaspoons Dijon mustard
¼ teaspoon olive oil
1 tablespoon minced capers
1 teaspoon sugar
1 teaspoon minced fresh garlic
¼ teaspoon ground black pepper

1 Combine orange juice, vinegar, parsley, mustard, oil, capers, sugar, garlic and black pepper in jar or bottle with tight-fitting lid; shake well. Refrigerate until ready to serve. Shake well before using.   *Makes ½ cup dressing*

SHRIMP-STUFFED ZUCCHINI ON THREE-PEPPER CONFETTI

Serve these colorful stuffed zucchini boats to enhance any dinner menu.

Nutrients per Serving:

Calories	154
(21% of calories from fat)	
Total Fat	4 g
Saturated Fat	1 g
Cholesterol	30 mg
Sodium	692 mg
Carbohydrate	22 g
Dietary Fiber	2 g
Protein	9 g
Calcium	101 mg
Iron	2 mg
Vitamin A	94 RE
Vitamin C	59 mg

DIETARY EXCHANGES:
1 Starch/Bread, ½ Lean
Meat, 1 Vegetable, ½ Fat

8 small zucchini, ends trimmed
4 ounces cooked baby shrimp
1½ cups Italian-seasoned dry bread crumbs
¼ cup freshly grated Parmesan cheese
¼ cup chopped green onions with tops
2 cloves garlic, minced
2 tablespoons minced fresh parsley
1 tablespoon olive oil
1 tablespoon chopped fresh savory, divided
¼ teaspoon ground black pepper
½ cup ⅓-less-salt chicken broth
⅔ cup diced red bell pepper
⅔ cup diced yellow bell pepper
⅔ cup diced green bell pepper

1 Preheat oven to 350°F. Slice zucchini in half lengthwise; scoop out pulp, leaving ¼-inch-thick shell. Finely chop zucchini pulp.

2 Combine chopped zucchini, shrimp, bread crumbs, Parmesan, onions, garlic, parsley, oil, 2 teaspoons savory and black pepper in medium bowl. Mix well.

3 Arrange zucchini shells in shallow baking dish. Stuff each zucchini shell with shrimp mixture. Bake 20 to 25 minutes or until golden brown.

4 Heat broth and remaining 1 teaspoon savory in small nonstick skillet. Bring to a boil over high heat. Add diced bell peppers. Cover and simmer 1 to 2 minutes or until peppers are crisp-tender.

5 For each serving, arrange zucchini boat over bed of mixed bell peppers. Garnish as desired.

Makes 8 servings

FRESH TOMATO EGGPLANT SPREAD

Studies have shown that eating eggplant may lower blood cholesterol levels and help counteract some of the effects that high fat foods have on the blood.

Nutrients per Serving:

Calories	117
(35% of calories from fat)	
Total Fat	4 g
Saturated Fat	0 g
Cholesterol	0 mg
Sodium	65 mg
Carbohydrate	15 g
Dietary Fiber	2 g
Protein	4 g
Calcium	13 mg
Iron	1 mg
Vitamin A	41 RE
Vitamin C	9 mg

DIETARY EXCHANGES:
3 Vegetable, 1 Fat

1 medium eggplant
2 large ripe tomatoes, seeded and chopped
1 cup minced zucchini
¼ cup chopped green onions with tops
2 tablespoons red wine vinegar
1 tablespoon olive oil
1 teaspoon honey
1 clove garlic, minced
1 tablespoon minced fresh basil
2 teaspoons minced fresh oregano
1 teaspoon minced fresh thyme
⅛ teaspoon ground black pepper
¼ cup pine nuts or slivered almonds
32 melba toast rounds

1 Preheat oven to 375°F. Poke holes in surface of eggplant with fork. Bake 20 to 25 minutes or until tender. Cool completely; peel and mince. Place in colander; press to release excess water.

2 Combine eggplant with tomatoes, zucchini, green onions, vinegar, oil, honey, garlic, basil, oregano, thyme and black pepper in large bowl. Mix well. Refrigerate 2 hours to allow flavors to blend.

3 Stir in pine nuts just before serving. Serve with melba toast rounds.

Makes 8 servings

MARINATED ANTIPASTO

This heart-healthy appetizer is loaded with vitamins A and C! It contains a plethora of fresh vegetables and herbs with only 13 percent of its calories from fat.

Nutrients per Serving:

Calories	61
(13% of calories from fat)	
Total Fat	1 g
Saturated Fat	0 g
Cholesterol	0 mg
Sodium	43 mg
Carbohydrate	13 g
Dietary Fiber	4 g
Protein	3 g
Calcium	60 mg
Iron	2 mg
Vitamin A	489 RE
Vitamin C	58 mg

DIETARY EXCHANGES:
2½ Vegetable

1 cup julienne-sliced carrots
1 cup fresh green beans, cut into 2-inch pieces
1 cup fresh brussels sprouts, quartered
1 cup thinly sliced baby yellow squash
1 can (9 ounces) artichoke hearts, drained, quartered
½ cup thinly sliced red bell pepper
½ cup thinly sliced yellow bell pepper
2 cups water
½ cup white wine vinegar
1 tablespoon olive oil
1 teaspoon sugar
2 bay leaves
1 clove garlic
6 sprigs fresh thyme
¼ teaspoon ground black pepper
½ cup chopped green onions with tops
½ cup minced parsley
   Peel of 2 oranges, cut into thin strips

1 Bring 4 cups water to a boil in large saucepan over high heat. Add carrots, beans, brussels sprouts, squash, artichoke hearts and bell peppers; cover and simmer 1 minute or until vegetables are crisp-tender. Remove from heat; drain. Place in heatproof bowl.

2 Combine 2 cups water, vinegar, oil, sugar, bay leaves, garlic, thyme and black pepper in medium saucepan. Bring to a boil over medium heat. Pour over vegetables; mix well. Cool completely. Cover and refrigerate 12 hours or up to 3 days before serving.

3 Before serving, drain vegetables. Discard bay leaves, garlic and thyme. Toss vegetables with onions, parsley and orange peel.

Makes 8 servings

ENTREES

FETTUCCINE GORGONZOLA WITH SUN-DRIED TOMATOES

Sun-dried tomatoes add their rich flavor to sauces, soups, sandwiches, salads and a myriad of other dishes.

8 ounces uncooked spinach or tri-color fettuccine
1 cup low fat cottage cheese
½ cup plain nonfat yogurt
½ cup (2 ounces) crumbled Gorgonzola cheese
⅛ teaspoon ground white pepper
2 cups rehydrated sun-dried tomatoes (4 ounces dry), cut into strips (see page 11)

1 Cook pasta according to package directions, omitting salt. Drain well. Cover to keep warm.

2 Combine cottage cheese and yogurt in food processor or blender; process until smooth. Heat cottage cheese mixture in small saucepan over low heat. Add Gorgonzola and white pepper; stir until cheese is melted.

3 Return pasta to saucepan; add tomatoes. Pour cheese mixture over pasta; mix well. Garnish as desired. Serve immediately.

Makes 4 servings

Nutrients per Serving:

Calories	358
(17% of calories from fat)	
Total Fat	7 g
Saturated Fat	4 g
Cholesterol	57 mg
Sodium	538 mg
Carbohydrate	55 g
Dietary Fiber	2 g
Protein	22 g
Calcium	251 mg
Iron	2 mg
Vitamin A	1540 RE
Vitamin C	35 mg

DIETARY EXCHANGES:
3½ Starch/Bread, 1½ Lean Meat, ½ Fat

Cook's Tip
Gorgonzola cheese is ivory-colored with thin or thick bluish-green veins throughout. This cheese is rich and creamy with a savory, slightly pungent flavor. Gorgonzola can be found in foil-wrapped wedges in most supermarkets.

SPINACH-STUFFED CHICKEN BREASTS

Like other greens, spinach is an excellent source of vitamin A in the form of beta-carotene, a powerful disease-fighting nutrient.

Nutrients per Serving:

Calories	187
(21% of calories from fat)	
Total Fat	4 g
Saturated Fat	2 g
Cholesterol	71 mg
Sodium	302 mg
Carbohydrate	10 g
Dietary Fiber	2 g
Protein	26 g
Calcium	115 mg
Iron	2 mg
Vitamin A	299 RE
Vitamin C	37 mg

DIETARY EXCHANGES:
3 Lean Meat, 1 Vegetable

2 boneless skinless chicken breasts (8 ounces each), halved
5 ounces frozen chopped spinach, thawed, well drained
2 tablespoons freshly grated Parmesan cheese
1 teaspoon grated lemon peel
¼ teaspoon ground black pepper
   Olive oil flavored nonstick cooking spray
1 cup thinly sliced mushrooms
6 slices (2 ounces) thinly sliced low fat turkey-ham
1 cup catawba juice*

1 Trim fat from chicken; discard. Place each chicken breast between 2 sheets of plastic wrap. Pound with meat mallet until chicken is about ¼ inch thick.

2 Preheat oven to 350°F. Pat spinach dry with paper towels. Combine spinach, Parmesan, lemon peel and black pepper in large bowl. Spray small nonstick skillet with cooking spray; add mushrooms. Cook and stir over medium heat 3 to 4 minutes or until tender.

3 Arrange 1½ slices turkey-ham over each chicken breast. Spread each with ¼ of spinach mixture. Top each with mushrooms. Beginning with longer side, roll chicken tightly. Tie with kitchen string.

4 Place stuffed chicken breasts in 9-inch square baking pan, seam side down. Lightly spray chicken with cooking spray. Pour catawba juice over top. Bake 30 minutes or until chicken is no longer pink.

5 Remove string; cut chicken rolls into ½-inch diagonal slices. Arrange on plate. Pour pan juices over chicken. Garnish as desired.   *Makes 4 servings*

*Or, substitute white grape juice.

VEAL IN GINGERED SWEET BELL PEPPER SAUCE

The delicate flavor and fine texture of veal have appealed to people for centuries. Serve this colorful main course with any one of our great vegetable side dishes.

Nutrients per Serving:	
Calories	120
(31% of calories from fat)	
Total Fat	4 g
Saturated Fat	1 g
Cholesterol	54 mg
Sodium	89 mg
Carbohydrate	6 g
Dietary Fiber	1 g
Protein	14 g
Calcium	62 mg
Iron	1 mg
Vitamin A	54 RE
Vitamin C	47 mg

DIETARY EXCHANGES:
2 Lean Meat, 1 Vegetable

1 teaspoon olive oil
¾ pound veal cutlets, thinly sliced
½ cup skim milk
1 tablespoon finely chopped fresh tarragon
2 teaspoons crushed capers
1 jar (7 ounces) roasted red peppers, drained
1 tablespoon lemon juice
½ teaspoon freshly grated ginger
½ teaspoon ground black pepper

1 Heat oil in medium saucepan over high heat. Add veal; lightly brown both sides. Reduce heat to medium. Add milk, chopped tarragon and capers. Cook, uncovered, 5 minutes or until veal is fork-tender and milk evaporates.

2 Place roasted peppers, lemon juice, ginger and black pepper in food processor or blender; process until smooth. Set aside.

3 Remove veal from pan with slotted spoon; place in serving dish. Spoon roasted pepper sauce over veal. Sprinkle with cooked capers and fresh tarragon, if desired.

Makes 4 servings

Health Note

All bell peppers have a great nutritional profile, but red bell peppers are the most nutritious. Roasted red peppers have high amounts of vitamins A and C and small amounts of calcium, phosphorus, iron, thiamin, riboflavin and niacin.

CIOPPINO

This tasty Italian fish stew is made with tomatoes and a variety of fish and shellfish.

Nutrients per Serving:	
Calories	214
(10% of calories from fat)	
Total Fat	2 g
Saturated Fat	0 g
Cholesterol	56 mg
Sodium	250 mg
Carbohydrate	27 g
Dietary Fiber	3 g
Protein	23 g
Calcium	132 mg
Iron	3 mg
Vitamin A	114 RE
Vitamin C	40 mg

DIETARY EXCHANGES:
1 Starch/Bread, 1½ Lean
Meat, 2 Vegetable

1 cup sliced onion
½ cup chopped celery
3 cloves garlic, minced
1 teaspoon olive oil
½ pound cod or other whitefish
½ pound bay or halved sea scallops
2 cups chopped unpeeled potatoes
1 can (28 ounces) no-salt-added stewed tomatoes
6 tablespoons chopped fresh parsley, divided
1 teaspoon dried oregano
1 tablespoon no-salt-added tomato paste
½ teaspoon ground black pepper
1 bay leaf
1 can (6 ounces) crabmeat

1 Place onion, celery, garlic and oil in large saucepan. Cook and stir over high heat until onion is tender; remove from pan with slotted spoon. Set aside.

2 Add cod, scallops and 2 cups water to same saucepan. Bring to a boil; simmer until cod flakes easily with fork. Remove seafood with slotted spoon. Set aside.

3 Return onion mixture to saucepan. Add potatoes, stewed tomatoes, 4 tablespoons parsley, oregano, tomato paste, black pepper and bay leaf. Bring to a boil over high heat; reduce heat to low. Simmer, uncovered, 15 minutes.

4 Add reserved cod, scallops and crabmeat to saucepan. Cover and cook 5 minutes. Remove bay leaf. Sprinkle with remaining 2 tablespoons parsley.   *Makes 6 servings*

FRESH VEGETABLE LASAGNA

This enticing lasagna recipe includes a layering of various fresh vegetables, which are naturally low in fat and sodium, yet supply plenty of fiber and flavor.

Nutrients per Serving:

Calories	250
(26% of calories from fat)	
Total Fat	8 g
Saturated Fat	4 g
Cholesterol	22 mg
Sodium	508 mg
Carbohydrate	26 g
Dietary Fiber	5 g
Protein	22 g
Calcium	401 mg
Iron	2 mg
Vitamin A	780 RE
Vitamin C	29 mg

DIETARY EXCHANGES:
1 Starch/Bread, 2 Lean
Meat, 2 Vegetable, ½ Fat

8 ounces uncooked lasagna noodles
1 package (10 ounces) frozen chopped spinach, thawed, well drained
1 cup shredded carrots
½ cup sliced green onions
½ cup sliced red bell pepper
¼ cup chopped fresh parsley
½ teaspoon ground black pepper
1½ cups low fat cottage cheese
1 cup buttermilk
½ cup plain nonfat yogurt
2 egg whites
1 cup sliced mushrooms
1 can (14 ounces) artichoke hearts, drained and chopped
2 cups (8 ounces) shredded part-skim mozzarella cheese
¼ cup freshly grated Parmesan cheese

1 Cook pasta according to package directions, omitting salt. Drain. Rinse under cold water; drain well. Set aside.

2 Preheat oven to 375°F. Pat spinach with paper towels to remove excess moisture. Combine spinach, carrots, green onions, bell pepper, parsley and black pepper in large bowl. Set aside.

3 Combine cottage cheese, buttermilk, yogurt and egg whites in food processor or blender; process until smooth.

4 Spray 13×9-inch baking pan with nonstick cooking spray. Arrange one-third of lasagna noodles in bottom of pan. Spread with half each of cottage cheese mixture, vegetable mixture, mushrooms, artichokes and mozzarella. Repeat layers, ending with noodles. Sprinkle with Parmesan.

5 Cover and bake 30 minutes. Remove cover; continue baking 20 minutes or until bubbly and heated through. Let stand 10 minutes before serving.

Makes 8 servings

PEASANT RISOTTO

This low fat dish is an Italian rice specialty made by adding warm broth to a mixture of rice, garlic, green onions and sage. The addition of Swiss chard gives it an extra nutritional boost.

1 teaspoon olive oil
3 ounces chopped low fat turkey-ham
2 cloves garlic, minced
1 cup arborio or white short-grain rice
1 can (15 ounces) Great Northern beans, rinsed and drained
¼ cup chopped green onions with tops
½ teaspoon dried sage leaves
2 cans (14 ounces each) ⅓-less-salt chicken broth, heated
1½ cups Swiss chard, rinsed, stems removed and shredded
¼ cup freshly grated Parmesan cheese

1 Heat oil in large saucepan over medium heat. Add turkey-ham and garlic. Cook and stir until garlic is browned. Add rice, beans, green onions and sage; blend well. Add warm broth; bring to a boil. Reduce heat to low. Cook about 25 minutes or until rice is creamy, stirring frequently.

2 Add Swiss chard and Parmesan; mix well. Cover; remove from heat. Let stand covered 2 minutes or until Swiss chard is wilted. Serve immediately.

Makes 4 servings

Nutrients per Serving:

Calories	372
(12% of calories from fat)	
Total Fat	5 g
Saturated Fat	2 g
Cholesterol	21 mg
Sodium	411 mg
Carbohydrate	63 g
Dietary Fiber	0 g
Protein	18 g
Calcium	162 mg
Iron	5 mg
Vitamin A	81 RE
Vitamin C	6 mg

DIETARY EXCHANGES:
4 Starch/Bread, 1 Lean Meat, ½ Fat

Health Note

Swiss chard, a member of the beet family, is treasured for its large leaves and celerylike stalks. It's exceptionally low in calories but high in vitamin A. Swiss chard contains enough vitamin E to be considered protective against certain types of cancers.

ZUCCHINI-TOMATO FRITTATA

"Frittata" is Italian for omelet. This dinner omelet is chock-full of fresh vegetables and has a sprinkling of Parmesan cheese.

❖

Nutrients per Serving:

Calories	160
(29% of calories from fat)	
Total Fat	5 g
Saturated Fat	2 g
Cholesterol	163 mg
Sodium	305 mg
Carbohydrate	13 g
Dietary Fiber	3 g
Protein	16 g
Calcium	120 mg
Iron	2 mg
Vitamin A	554 RE
Vitamin C	84 mg

DIETARY EXCHANGES:
2 Lean Meat,
1½ Vegetable

1 cup sliced zucchini
1 cup broccoli flowerets
1 cup diced red or yellow bell peppers
3 whole eggs, lightly beaten*
5 egg whites, lightly beaten*
½ cup low fat cottage cheese
½ cup rehydrated sun-dried tomatoes (1 ounce dry), coarsely chopped
    (see page 11)
¼ cup chopped green onions with tops
¼ cup chopped fresh basil
⅛ teaspoon ground red pepper
2 tablespoons Parmesan cheese

1 Preheat broiler. Spray 10-inch ovenproof nonstick skillet with olive oil flavored nonstick cooking spray. Place zucchini, broccoli and bell peppers in skillet; cook and stir over high heat 3 to 4 minutes or until crisp-tender.

2 Combine whole eggs, egg whites, cottage cheese, tomatoes, onions, basil and ground red pepper in medium bowl. Mix well. Pour egg mixture over vegetables in skillet. Cook, uncovered, gently lifting sides of frittata so uncooked egg flows underneath. Cook 7 to 8 minutes or until frittata is almost firm and golden brown on bottom. Remove from heat. Sprinkle with Parmesan.

3 Broil about 5 inches from heat 3 to 5 minutes or until golden brown on surface. Garnish with paprika, if desired. Cut into wedges. Serve immediately.

Makes 4 servings

*Or, substitute cholesterol free egg substitute to equal 6 large eggs.

HERBED SCALLOPS AND SHRIMP

Shellfish are naturally low in saturated fat and provide a dose of healthy omega-3 fatty acids, which are believed to help reduce the risk of heart disease.

Nutrients per Serving:

Calories	152
(27% of calories from fat)	
Total Fat	5 g
Saturated Fat	1 g
Cholesterol	111 mg
Sodium	223 mg
Carbohydrate	8 g
Dietary Fiber	0 g
Protein	20 g
Calcium	95 mg
Iron	3 mg
Vitamin A	79 RE
Vitamin C	16 mg

DIETARY EXCHANGES:
2½ Lean Meat,
1 Vegetable

¼ cup chopped fresh parsley
¼ cup lime juice
2 tablespoons chopped fresh mint
2 tablespoons chopped fresh rosemary
1 tablespoon honey
1 tablespoon olive oil
2 cloves garlic, minced
¼ teaspoon ground black pepper
½ pound raw jumbo shrimp, peeled and deveined
½ pound bay or halved sea scallops

1 Preheat broiler. Combine parsley, lime juice, mint, rosemary, honey, oil, garlic and black pepper in medium bowl; blend well. Add shrimp and scallops. Cover; refrigerate 1 hour.

2 Arrange shrimp and scallops on skewers. Place on broiler pan. Brush with marinade. Broil 5 to 6 minutes or until shrimp are opaque and scallops are lightly browned. Serve immediately with lime slices and fresh mint sprigs, if desired.

Makes 4 servings

Cook's Tip
To store fresh mint, place in a glass of water; refrigerate. Be sure to change the water daily, and try to use mint within three to four days.

FUSILLI PIZZAIOLA WITH TURKEY MEATBALLS

If you crave pasta and meatballs, this home-style dish will hit the spot!

Nutrients per Serving:

Calories	330
(27% of calories from fat)	
Total Fat	10 g
Saturated Fat	2 g
Cholesterol	116 mg
Sodium	111 mg
Carbohydrate	39 g
Dietary Fiber	3 g
Protein	21 g
Calcium	54 mg
Iron	4 mg
Vitamin A	65 RE
Vitamin C	48 mg

DIETARY EXCHANGES:
2 Starch/Bread, ½ Fat,
2 Lean Meat, 2 Vegetable

1 pound ground turkey breast
1 egg, lightly beaten
1 tablespoon skim milk
¼ cup Italian-seasoned dry bread crumbs
2 tablespoons chopped fresh parsley
¼ teaspoon ground black pepper, divided
½ cup chopped onion
½ cup grated carrots
1 clove garlic, minced
2 teaspoons olive oil
2 cans (14½ ounces each) no-salt-added whole tomatoes, undrained
2 tablespoons chopped fresh basil
1 tablespoon no-salt-added tomato paste
½ teaspoon dried thyme leaves
1 bay leaf
8 ounces uncooked fusilli or other spiral-shaped pasta

1 Preheat oven to 350°F. Combine turkey, egg and milk in medium bowl. Add bread crumbs, parsley and ⅛ teaspoon black pepper; mix well. With wet hands, shape turkey mixture into small balls.

2 Spray baking sheet with nonstick cooking spray. Arrange meatballs on baking sheet. Bake 25 minutes or until no longer pink in center.

3 Place onion, carrots, garlic and oil in medium saucepan. Cook and stir over high heat 5 minutes or until onion is tender. Add tomatoes, basil, tomato paste, thyme, bay leaf and remaining ⅛ teaspoon black pepper. Bring to a boil; reduce heat to low. Simmer 25 minutes; add meatballs. Cover, simmer 5 to 10 minutes or until sauce thickens slightly. Remove bay leaf.

4 Cook pasta according to package directions, omitting salt. Drain well. Place in large serving bowl. Spoon meatballs and sauce over pasta. Garnish as desired.

Makes 4 servings

ANGEL HAIR PASTA WITH SEAFOOD SAUCE

Angel hair pasta is best served with a thin, delicate sauce such as this irresistible one which uses fresh plum tomatoes and savory seafood.

Nutrients per Serving:

Calories	272
(15% of calories from fat)	
Total Fat	5 g
Saturated Fat	1 g
Cholesterol	31 mg
Sodium	134 mg
Carbohydrate	38 g
Dietary Fiber	5 g
Protein	21 g
Calcium	75 mg
Iron	4 mg
Vitamin A	189 RE
Vitamin C	47 mg

DIETARY EXCHANGES:
2 Starch/Bread, 1½ Lean
Meat, 2 Vegetable

½ pound firm whitefish, such as sea bass, monkfish or grouper
2 teaspoons olive oil
½ cup chopped onion
2 cloves garlic, minced
3 pounds fresh plum tomatoes, seeded and chopped
¼ cup chopped fresh basil
2 tablespoons chopped fresh oregano
1 teaspoon crushed red pepper
½ teaspoon sugar
2 bay leaves
½ pound fresh bay scallops or shucked oysters
8 ounces uncooked angel hair pasta
2 tablespoons chopped fresh parsley

1 Cut whitefish into ¾-inch pieces. Set aside.

2 Heat oil in large nonstick skillet over medium heat; add onion and garlic. Cook and stir 3 minutes or until onion is tender. Reduce heat to low; add tomatoes, basil, oregano, crushed red pepper, sugar and bay leaves. Cook, uncovered, 15 minutes, stirring occasionally.

3 Add whitefish and scallops. Cook, uncovered, 3 to 4 minutes or until fish flakes easily when tested with fork and scallops are opaque. Remove bay leaves; discard. Set seafood sauce aside.

4 Cook pasta according to package directions, omitting salt. Drain well.

5 Combine pasta with seafood sauce in large serving bowl. Mix well. Sprinkle with parsley. Serve immediately. *Makes 6 servings*

ROASTED PEPPER PIZZA

One of the latest food trends is gourmet pizzas. This tasty pizza is topped with fresh tomatoes, basil, parsley, roasted peppers, mushrooms and blue cheese.

1 cup chopped fresh tomatoes
¼ cup fresh basil
¼ cup fresh parsley
2 tablespoons fresh oregano
2 tablespoons no-salt-added tomato paste
1 teaspoon olive oil
1 clove garlic
¼ teaspoon ground black pepper
6 (6-inch) whole wheat pita breads
1 jar (8 ounces) roasted red peppers, drained and sliced
1½ cups sliced mushrooms
1½ cups (6 ounces) shredded part-skim mozzarella cheese
¼ cup crumbled blue cheese

1 Preheat oven to 425°F.

2 Place tomatoes, basil, parsley, oregano, tomato paste, oil, garlic and black pepper in food processor or blender; process until smooth.

3 Arrange pita breads on ungreased baking sheet; spread tomato mixture over pitas. Top with roasted peppers, mushrooms, mozzarella and blue cheese.

4 Bake 7 to 10 minutes or until pitas are lightly browned on bottoms and cheese is melted. Garnish as desired. *Makes 6 servings*

Nutrients per Serving:

Calories	299
(26% of calories from fat)	
Total Fat	9 g
Saturated Fat	4 g
Cholesterol	20 mg
Sodium	560 mg
Carbohydrate	43 g
Dietary Fiber	2 g
Protein	16 g
Calcium	246 mg
Iron	1 mg
Vitamin A	138 RE
Vitamin C	47 mg

DIETARY EXCHANGES:
2 Starch/Bread, 1 Lean Meat, 2 Vegetable, 1 Fat

ROASTED ROSEMARY-LEMON CHICKEN

Cooking poultry with the skin on insulates the poultry, keeping it tender and moist. Removing the skin just before serving reduces fat almost as much as cooking poultry skinless.

Nutrients per Serving:

Calories	282
(33% of calories from fat)	
Total Fat	10 g
Saturated Fat	3 g
Cholesterol	120 mg
Sodium	133 mg
Carbohydrate	6 g
Dietary Fiber	1 g
Protein	40 g
Calcium	40 mg
Iron	2 mg
Vitamin A	544 RE
Vitamin C	6 mg

DIETARY EXCHANGES:
5 Lean Meat, 1 Vegetable

1 whole chicken (3¼ pounds)
½ teaspoon ground black pepper
1 lemon, cut into eighths
¼ cup fresh parsley
4 sprigs fresh rosemary
3 fresh sage leaves
2 sprigs fresh thyme
1 can (14 ounces) ⅓-less-salt chicken broth
1 cup sliced onions
4 cloves garlic
1 cup thinly sliced carrots
1 cup thinly sliced zucchini

1 Preheat oven to 350°F. Trim fat from chicken, leaving skin on. Rinse chicken and pat dry with paper towels. Fill cavity of chicken with black pepper, lemon, parsley, rosemary, sage and thyme. Close cavity with skewers.

2 Combine broth, onions and garlic in heavy roasting pan. Place chicken in broth. Bake 1½ hours or until juices run clear when pierced with fork. Remove chicken to cutting board.

3 Combine carrots and zucchini in small saucepan with tight-fitting lid. Add ¼ cup water; bring to a boil over high heat. Reduce heat to medium. Cover and steam 4 minutes or until vegetables are crisp-tender. Transfer vegetables to colander; drain.

4 Remove skewers. Discard lemon and herbs from cavity of chicken. Remove skin from chicken. Cut chicken into pieces; place on medium serving plate. Remove onions and garlic from pan with slotted spoon to large bowl. Add carrots and zucchini; mix well. Arrange vegetable mixture around chicken. Garnish with fresh rosemary and lemon, if desired.

Makes 6 servings

VEGETABLES & SIDES

COUNTRY GREEN BEANS WITH HAM

Green beans mixed with tomatoes are an old Italian favorite. Add smoked ham, fresh herbs and spices and you've created an exquisite side dish.

2 teaspoons olive oil
¼ cup minced onion
1 clove garlic, minced
1 pound fresh green beans, rinsed and drained
1 cup chopped fresh tomatoes
6 slices (2 ounces) thinly sliced low fat smoked turkey-ham
1 tablespoon chopped fresh marjoram
2 teaspoons chopped fresh basil
⅛ teaspoon ground black pepper
¼ cup herbed croutons

1 Heat oil in medium saucepan over medium heat. Add onion and garlic; cook and stir about 3 minutes or until onion is tender. Reduce heat to low.

2 Add green beans, tomatoes, turkey-ham, marjoram, basil and black pepper. Cook about 10 minutes, stirring occasionally, until liquid from tomato is absorbed.

3 Transfer mixture to serving dish. Top with croutons.   *Makes 4 servings*

Nutrients per Serving:	
Calories	100
(27% of calories from fat)	
Total Fat	3 g
Saturated Fat	1 g
Cholesterol	12 mg
Sodium	194 mg
Carbohydrate	14 g
Dietary Fiber	4 g
Protein	6 g
Calcium	66 mg
Iron	2 mg
Vitamin A	110 RE
Vitamin C	22 mg

DIETARY EXCHANGES:
3 Vegetable, ½ Fat

Cook's Tip
Select fresh green beans that are firm, smooth and brightly colored. They should be crisp enough to snap when bent in half. Avoid those that are discolored, spotted or leathery looking.

ZUCCHINI TOMATO BAKE

In this vegetable dish, zucchini is baked with eggplant, tomatoes, mushrooms, onion, fennel and garlic to create an elegant low fat accompaniment to any entrée.

1 pound eggplant, coarsely chopped
2 cups thinly sliced zucchini
2 cups sliced fresh mushrooms
2 teaspoons olive oil
½ cup chopped onion
½ cup chopped fresh fennel
2 cloves garlic, minced
1 can (14½ ounces) no-salt-added whole tomatoes, undrained
1 tablespoon no-salt-added tomato paste
2 teaspoons dried basil leaves
1 teaspoon sugar

1 Preheat oven to 350°F. Arrange eggplant, zucchini and mushrooms in 9-inch square baking dish.

2 Heat oil in small skillet over medium heat. Cook and stir onion, fennel and garlic 3 to 4 minutes or until onion is tender. Add tomatoes, tomato paste, basil and sugar. Cook and stir about 4 minutes or until sauce thickens.

3 Pour sauce over eggplant mixture. Cover and bake 30 minutes. Cool slightly before serving. Garnish as desired.

Makes 6 servings

Nutrients per Serving:

Calories	71
(23% of calories from fat)	
Total Fat	2 g
Saturated Fat	0 g
Cholesterol	0 mg
Sodium	39 mg
Carbohydrate	13 g
Dietary Fiber	3 g
Protein	3 g
Calcium	50 mg
Iron	1 mg
Vitamin A	71 RE
Vitamin C	19 mg

DIETARY EXCHANGES:
2 Vegetable, ½ Fat

Cook's Tip

Eggplant is available year-round. Choose a firm, smooth-skinned eggplant that is heavy for its size. Try to avoid those with soft spots. Store them in a cool, dry place and use within a day or two of purchase.

POLENTA LASAGNA

Polenta, a staple of northern Italy, is made from cornmeal. In this low fat dish, it is flavored with a variety of herbs, vegetables and cheeses.

Nutrients per Serving:

Calories	201
(19% of calories from fat)	
Total Fat	5 g
Saturated Fat	1 g
Cholesterol	7 mg
Sodium	148 mg
Carbohydrate	34 g
Dietary Fiber	7 g
Protein	9 g
Calcium	91 mg
Iron	3 mg
Vitamin A	44 RE
Vitamin C	28 mg

DIETARY EXCHANGES:
2 Starch/Bread,
1½ Vegetable, ½ Fat

4¼ cups water, divided
1½ cups whole grain yellow cornmeal
4 teaspoons finely chopped fresh marjoram
1 teaspoon olive oil
1 pound fresh mushrooms, sliced
1 cup chopped leeks
1 clove garlic, minced
½ cup (2 ounces) shredded part-skim mozzarella cheese
2 tablespoons chopped fresh basil
1 tablespoon chopped fresh oregano
⅛ teaspoon ground black pepper
2 red bell peppers, chopped
¼ cup freshly grated Parmesan cheese, divided

1 Bring 4 cups water to a boil in medium saucepan over high heat. Slowly add cornmeal to water, stirring constantly with wire whisk. Reduce heat to low; stir in marjoram. Simmer 15 to 20 minutes or until polenta thickens and pulls away from side of saucepan. Spread on 13×9-inch ungreased baking sheet. Chill about 1 hour or until firm.

2 Heat oil in medium nonstick skillet over medium heat. Add mushrooms, leeks and garlic; cook and stir 5 minutes or until vegetables are crisp-tender. Stir in mozzarella, basil, oregano and black pepper.

3 Place bell peppers and remaining ¼ cup water in food processor or blender; process until smooth. Preheat oven to 350°F. Spray 11×7-inch baking dish with nonstick cooking spray.

4 Cut cold polenta into 12 (3½-inch) squares; arrange 6 squares in bottom of prepared pan. Spread with half of bell pepper mixture, half of vegetable mixture and 2 tablespoons Parmesan. Place remaining 6 squares polenta over Parmesan; top with remaining bell pepper and vegetable mixtures and Parmesan. Bake 20 minutes or until cheese is melted and polenta is golden brown. Garnish as desired.

Makes 6 servings

FENNEL WITH PARMESAN BREAD CRUMBS

Fennel is a celerylike stalk with an anise flavor. It is enjoyed raw in salads or cooked as a side dish or in soups. Its leaves are often used as an herb in salads, stuffings and sauces.

Nutrients per Serving:

Calories	113
(31% of calories from fat)	
Total Fat	4 g
Saturated Fat	1 g
Cholesterol	1 mg
Sodium	213 mg
Carbohydrate	16 g
Dietary Fiber	0 g
Protein	3 g
Calcium	76 mg
Iron	1 mg
Vitamin A	5 RE
Vitamin C	13 mg

DIETARY EXCHANGES:
1 Starch/Bread, 1 Fat

2 large fennel bulbs
½ cup dry bread crumbs
¼ cup lemon juice
1 tablespoon freshly grated Parmesan cheese
1 tablespoon capers
2 teaspoons olive oil
⅛ teaspoon ground black pepper
½ cup ⅓-less-salt chicken broth

1 Preheat oven to 375°F. Spray 9-inch square baking dish with nonstick cooking spray; set aside.

2 Remove outer leaves and wide base from fennel bulbs. Slice bulbs crosswise.

3 Combine fennel and ¼ cup water in medium nonstick skillet with tight-fitting lid. Bring to a boil over high heat; reduce heat to medium. Cover and steam 4 minutes or until fennel is crisp-tender. Cool slightly; arrange in prepared baking pan.

4 Combine bread crumbs, lemon juice, Parmesan, capers, oil and black pepper in small bowl. Sprinkle bread crumb mixture over fennel; pour broth over top.

5 Bake, uncovered, 20 to 25 minutes or until golden brown. Garnish with chopped fennel leaves and red bell pepper strips, if desired.   *Makes 4 servings*

Cook's Tip
Choosing fresh fennel is easy. Select clean, crisp bulbs with no sign of browning. Any greenery should be a fresh green color. To store fennel, refrigerate it tightly wrapped in a plastic food storage bag for up to five days.

SPICY PARSLEY SAUCE WITH ANGEL HAIR PASTA

This delicious sauce is served over angel hair pasta—feel free to substitute your favorite thin noodle for the angel hair. If the level of spice is too much for you, simply decrease the amount of chili peppers and hot pepper sauce.

Nutrients per Serving:

Calories	146
(30% of calories from fat)	
Total Fat	5 g
Saturated Fat	1 g
Cholesterol	0 mg
Sodium	11 mg
Carbohydrate	21 g
Dietary Fiber	2 g
Protein	5 g
Calcium	26 mg
Iron	2 mg
Vitamin A	45 RE
Vitamin C	18 mg

DIETARY EXCHANGES:
1 Starch/Bread,
1 Vegetable, 1 Fat

1 cup chopped fresh parsley
2 fresh red chili peppers, seeded and chopped*
   Dash hot red pepper sauce
1 clove garlic, minced
2 tablespoons lemon juice
1 teaspoon grated lemon peel
⅛ teaspoon ground black pepper
4 teaspoons olive oil
¼ cup slivered almonds
1 teaspoon cornstarch
½ cup ⅓-less-salt chicken broth
½ pound uncooked angel hair pasta

1 Combine parsley, chili peppers, hot pepper sauce, garlic, lemon juice, lemon peel and black pepper in medium bowl. Blend well. Mix in oil and almonds.

2 Combine cornstarch and broth in small saucepan. Cook and stir over low heat 3 to 5 minutes or until thickened. Remove from heat; add to parsley mixture.

3 Cook pasta according to package directions, omitting salt. Drain well. Transfer to large serving bowl. Pour parsley sauce over pasta; mix well. Garnish as desired.

Makes 8 servings

*Wear rubber gloves when handling chili peppers. Do not touch your face while handling chilies and wash your hands well in soapy warm water after handling chilies to remove any oils.

TOMATO-ARTICHOKE FOCACCIA

*This delicious, healthy
focaccia can be eaten as a
snack or served as an
accompaniment to any soup
or salad.*

Nutrients per Serving:

Calories	160
(30% of calories from fat)	
Total Fat	5 g
Saturated Fat	1 g
Cholesterol	2 mg
Sodium	143 mg
Carbohydrate	24 g
Dietary Fiber	1 g
Protein	4 g
Calcium	43 mg
Iron	1 mg
Vitamin A	95 RE
Vitamin C	4 mg

DIETARY EXCHANGES:
1½ Starch/Bread,
½ Vegetable, 1 Fat

1 package (16 ounces) hot roll mix
2 tablespoons wheat bran
1¼ cups hot water
4 teaspoons olive oil, divided
1 cup thinly sliced onions
2 cloves garlic, minced
1 cup rehydrated sun-dried tomatoes (4 ounces dry), cut into strips (see page 11)
1 cup artichoke hearts, sliced
1 tablespoon minced fresh rosemary
2 tablespoons freshly grated Parmesan cheese

1 Preheat oven to 400°F. Combine dry ingredients and yeast packet from hot roll mix in large bowl. Add bran; mix well. Stir in hot water and 2 teaspoons oil. Knead dough about 5 minutes or until ingredients are blended.

2 Spray 15½×11½-inch baking pan or 14-inch pizza pan with nonstick cooking spray. Press dough onto bottom of prepared pan. Cover; let rise 15 minutes.

3 Heat 1 teaspoon oil in medium skillet over low heat. Add onions and garlic; cook and stir 2 to 3 minutes or until onions are tender.

4 Brush surface of dough with remaining teaspoon oil. Top dough with onion mixture, tomatoes, artichokes and fresh rosemary. Sprinkle with Parmesan.

5 Bake 25 to 30 minutes or until lightly browned on top. Cut into squares. Garnish each square with fresh rosemary sprigs, if desired.   *Makes 16 servings*

LEMON-GARLIC BROCCOLI OVER SPAGHETTI SQUASH

Spaghetti squash makes a great substitute for pasta and offers an easy way to add a vegetable serving to a meal! One cup of spaghetti squash has just 33 calories, 1 gram of fat, 1 milligram of sodium and 4 grams of fiber.

Nutrients per Serving:

Calories	44
(13% of calories from fat)	
Total Fat	1 g
Saturated Fat	0 g
Cholesterol	0 mg
Sodium	11 mg
Carbohydrate	10 g
Dietary Fiber	3 g
Protein	3 g
Calcium	59 mg
Iron	1 mg
Vitamin A	81 RE
Vitamin C	38 mg

DIETARY EXCHANGES:
2 Vegetable

1 spaghetti squash (2 pounds)
1 can (14 ounces) ⅓-less-salt chicken broth
10 large cloves garlic, halved
2 tablespoons lemon juice
3 fresh sage leaves
2 cups broccoli flowerets

1 Place spaghetti squash in large saucepan. Pierce skin with fork. Add enough water to cover. Bring to a boil over high heat. Reduce heat to low; simmer, covered, 20 to 30 minutes or until squash is soft. Cut squash in half lengthwise; remove seeds. Set aside.

2 Combine broth and garlic in small saucepan. Bring to a boil over high heat. Reduce heat to low; simmer, uncovered, 15 minutes or until garlic is tender. Remove from heat; cool slightly.

3 Place broth, garlic, lemon juice and sage in food processor or blender; process until smooth. Return mixture to saucepan to keep warm.

4 Combine broccoli and ¼ cup water in large nonstick skillet with tight-fitting lid. Bring to a boil over high heat. Reduce heat to medium. Cover and steam 5 minutes or until broccoli is crisp-tender.

5 Scoop out inside of squash with fork. Place squash and broccoli in medium bowl; pour lemon-garlic mixture over squash mixture. Mix well. Garnish as desired. Serve immediately.

Makes 6 servings

SAUCES

SPICY TOMATO SAUCE

Serve this hearty sauce with thick fettucine noodles or hefty rigatoni and Salad Primavera (page 26) for a perfect meal.

1 teaspoon olive oil
2 ounces Canadian bacon, cut into thin strips
¼ cup chopped onion
2 cloves garlic, minced
½ pound fresh mushrooms, sliced
2 cans (14 ounces each) no-salt-added whole tomatoes, undrained
2 tablespoons chopped fresh parsley
1 teaspoon dried oregano leaves
½ teaspoon crushed red pepper
⅛ teaspoon ground black pepper

 Heat oil in medium saucepan over high heat. Stir in bacon, onion and garlic. Cook and stir 3 minutes or until onion is tender. Add mushrooms; cook and stir 2 minutes or until mushrooms are tender.

 Add tomatoes, parsley, oregano, crushed red pepper and black pepper to saucepan. Bring to a boil; cover. Simmer 50 to 60 minutes over medium heat, stirring occasionally, until sauce thickens. Garnish as desired.   *Makes 6 (½-cup) servings*

Nutrients per Serving:

Calories	59
(25% of calories from fat)	
Total Fat	2 g
Saturated Fat	0 g
Cholesterol	3 mg
Sodium	111 mg
Carbohydrate	9 g
Dietary Fiber	2 g
Protein	4 g
Calcium	46 mg
Iron	2 mg
Vitamin A	94 RE
Vitamin C	25 mg

DIETARY EXCHANGES:
2 Vegetable

Health Note

The news is out: Research shows that monounsaturated fat, like that found in olive oil, helps to lower total cholesterol. Other studies suggest that olive oil may significantly lower blood pressure.

MUSHROOM-CLAM SAUCE

Serve this light, flavorful sauce over a thin pasta, such as vermicelli or angel hair.

½ cup chopped onion
3 cloves garlic, minced
1 tablespoon olive oil, divided
1 pint shucked fresh clams, drained and chopped
1 bottle (8 ounces) clam juice
2 tablespoons lemon juice
½ cup chopped fresh parsley
½ teaspoon dried marjoram leaves
⅛ teaspoon ground black pepper
¼ pound portabello mushrooms, sliced
½ cup dry white wine
2 teaspoons cornstarch

1 Place onion, garlic and 1 teaspoon oil in large heavy saucepan. Cook and stir over medium heat 3 minutes or until onion is tender. Stir in clams, clam juice, lemon juice, parsley, marjoram and black pepper. Bring to a boil; reduce heat. Simmer, uncovered, 10 minutes or until clams are tender.

2 Combine mushrooms and remaining 2 teaspoons oil in small saucepan. Cook and stir until mushrooms are tender. Set aside.

3 Blend wine and cornstarch in small bowl until smooth. Add to clam mixture; mix well. Simmer 1 minute or until thickened. Mix in mushrooms just before serving.

Makes 8 (¼-cup) servings

Nutrients per Serving:	
Calories	86
(24% of calories from fat)	
Total Fat	2 g
Saturated Fat	0 g
Cholesterol	19 mg
Sodium	72 mg
Carbohydrate	6 g
Dietary Fiber	1 g
Protein	8 g
Calcium	38 mg
Iron	8 mg
Vitamin A	67 RE
Vitamin C	14 mg

DIETARY EXCHANGES:
1 Lean Meat, 1 Vegetable

NEAPOLITAN SAUCE

This flavorful red sauce comes straight from Naples, Italy, where parsley and basil are considered staple ingredients in any great pasta sauce.

½ cup minced green bell pepper
¼ cup minced onion
¼ cup coarsely chopped celery
2 cloves garlic, minced
1 teaspoon olive oil
2 cans (10 ounces each) no-salt-added whole tomatoes, undrained
¼ cup chopped fresh parsley
1 tablespoon chopped fresh basil
¼ teaspoon salt
⅛ teaspoon ground black pepper

1 Place bell pepper, onion, celery, garlic and oil in medium saucepan. Cook and stir over medium heat until onion is tender.

2 Add tomatoes, parsley, basil, salt and black pepper. Reduce heat to low; cover. Simmer 15 minutes; uncover. Cook and stir 10 minutes or until sauce thickens.

Makes 8 (½-cup) servings

Nutrients per Serving:

Calories	36
(20% of calories from fat)	
Total Fat	1 g
Saturated Fat	0 g
Cholesterol	0 mg
Sodium	86 mg
Carbohydrate	7 g
Dietary Fiber	1 g
Protein	1 g
Calcium	38 mg
Iron	1 mg
Vitamin A	87 RE
Vitamin C	33 mg

DIETARY EXCHANGES:
1½ Vegetable

Health Note
Parsley is a very low-calorie source of vitamins A and C for protection against cancer. It also contains potassium for healthy blood pressure, and calcium for strong bones.

TOMATO-SAGE SAUCE

Sage, a native Mediterranean herb, has been enjoyed for centuries for both its culinary and medicinal uses. The name is Latin (meaning "safe") and is a reference to the healing powers once attributed to the herb.

2 cans (10 ounces each) no-salt-added whole tomatoes, undrained
1 teaspoon olive oil
3 cloves garlic, minced
¼ cup chopped fresh parsley
2 tablespoons chopped fresh sage
2 teaspoons sugar
¼ teaspoon ground black pepper

1 Place tomatoes in food processor or blender; process until finely chopped. Set aside.

2 Heat oil in medium saucepan over low heat. Add tomatoes, garlic, parsley, sage, sugar and black pepper. Cook over medium heat 30 minutes or until thickened.

Makes 8 (¼-cup) servings

Nutrients per Serving:

Calories	32
(21% of calories from fat)	
Total Fat	1 g
Saturated Fat	0 g
Cholesterol	0 mg
Sodium	14 mg
Carbohydrate	6 g
Dietary Fiber	1 g
Protein	1 g
Calcium	34 mg
Iron	1 mg
Vitamin A	70 RE
Vitamin C	18 mg

DIETARY EXCHANGES:
1½ Vegetable

Cook's Tip

Small bunches of fresh sage are available year-round in many supermarkets. Choose fresh sage by its color and aroma. Store sage refrigerated wrapped in paper towels and sealed in a resealable plastic food storage bag for up to four days.

TURKEY BOLOGNESE SAUCE

Try this chunky sauce in place of your normal pasta sauce made with ground beef. It's much lower in fat and the vegetables add a healthy twist.

❖

Nutrients per Serving:

Calories	94
(27% of calories from fat)	
Total Fat	3 g
Saturated Fat	1 g
Cholesterol	17 mg
Sodium	145 mg
Carbohydrate	9 g
Dietary Fiber	2 g
Protein	9 g
Calcium	52 mg
Iron	1 mg
Vitamin A	262 RE
Vitamin C	21 mg

DIETARY EXCHANGES:
1 Lean Meat,
1½ Vegetable

½ cup chopped onion
½ cup chopped carrots
½ cup chopped celery
¼ cup chopped green bell pepper
2 ounces Canadian bacon, chopped
2 cloves garlic, minced
1 tablespoon olive oil
½ pound ground turkey breast
½ cup ⅓-less-salt chicken broth
1 can (10 ounces) no-salt-added whole tomatoes, undrained
¼ cup no-salt-added tomato paste
1 bay leaf
¼ teaspoon grated nutmeg
⅛ teaspoon ground black pepper
½ pound fresh mushrooms, sliced
½ cup 1% low fat milk

1 Place onion, carrots, celery, bell pepper, bacon and garlic in large saucepan. Add oil; cook and stir over medium heat 5 minutes or until vegetables are tender.

2 Add turkey; cook and stir until completely browned. Add broth, tomatoes, tomato paste, bay leaf, nutmeg and black pepper. Bring to a boil over high heat; cover and reduce heat to medium. Simmer 45 minutes, stirring occasionally. Uncover; simmer 15 minutes.

3 Add mushrooms; simmer 10 minutes. Stir in milk; simmer 5 minutes. Remove bay leaf before serving.

Makes 8 servings

DESSERTS

MINTED PEARS WITH GORGONZOLA

Pears are a great source of copper, potassium, vitamin C, boron and fiber. You can find fresh pears starting in late summer and continuing through the winter.

4 whole firm pears with stems, peeled
2 cups Concord grape juice
1 tablespoon honey
1 tablespoon finely chopped fresh mint
1 cinnamon stick
¼ teaspoon ground nutmeg
¼ cup Gorgonzola cheese, crumbled

1 Place pears in medium saucepan. Add grape juice, honey, mint, cinnamon stick and nutmeg. Bring to a boil over high heat. Cover and simmer 15 to 20 minutes, turning pears once to absorb juices evenly. Cook until pears can be easily pierced with fork. Remove from heat; cool. Remove pears with slotted spoon to serving plates; set aside. Discard cinnamon stick.

2 Bring juice mixture to a boil; simmer 20 minutes. Pour over pears. Sprinkle Gorgonzola around pears. Garnish as desired.

Makes 4 servings

Nutrients per Serving:

Calories	194
(13% of calories from fat)	
Total Fat	3 g
Saturated Fat	2 g
Cholesterol	6 mg
Sodium	119 mg
Carbohydrate	42 g
Dietary Fiber	4 g
Protein	2 g
Calcium	68 mg
Iron	1 mg
Vitamin A	31 RE
Vitamin C	28 mg

DIETARY EXCHANGES:
2½ Fruit, 1 Fat

Health Note
Grape juice has fairly good amounts of vitamins A and C to help protect from colds and flu. It is also a good source of potassium and relatively low in sodium.

POLENTA APRICOT PUDDING CAKE

Polenta, a popular main course or side dish, also makes a traditional base for desserts. This very moist country cake is made more nutritious with vitamin-A-rich apricots and calcium-rich ricotta cheese.

Nutrients per Serving:

Calories	245
(17% of calories from fat)	
Total Fat	5 g
Saturated Fat	2 g
Cholesterol	10 mg
Sodium	43 mg
Carbohydrate	48 g
Dietary Fiber	3 g
Protein	6 g
Calcium	104 mg
Iron	1 mg
Vitamin A	85 RE
Vitamin C	31 mg

DIETARY EXCHANGES:
2½ Starch/Bread, 1 Fat

¼ cup chopped dried apricots
2 cups orange juice
1 cup part-skim ricotta cheese
3 tablespoons honey
¾ cup sugar
½ cup cornmeal
½ cup all-purpose flour
¼ teaspoon grated nutmeg
¼ cup slivered almonds

1 Preheat oven to 300°F. Soak apricots in ¼ cup water in small bowl 15 minutes. Drain and discard water. Pat apricots dry with paper towels; set aside.

2 Combine orange juice, ricotta cheese and honey in medium bowl. Mix on medium speed of electric mixer 5 minutes or until smooth. Combine sugar, cornmeal, flour and nutmeg in small bowl. Gradually add sugar mixture to orange juice mixture; blend well. Slowly stir in apricots.

3 Spray 10-inch nonstick springform pan with nonstick cooking spray. Pour batter into prepared pan. Sprinkle with almonds. Bake 60 to 70 minutes or until center is firm and cake is golden brown. Garnish with powdered sugar, if desired. Serve warm.

Makes 8 servings

Health Note

Apricots are packed with beta-carotene and fiber to help prevent cancer. Apricots are also high in potassium and low in sodium to help with blood pressure control.

TIRAMISU

Instead of mascarpone cheese, egg yolks and cognac, this low fat version of tiramisu is prepared with a spectacular spiced custard, and flavored with orange extract.

Nutrients per Serving:	
Calories	223
(19% of calories from fat)	
Total Fat	5 g
Saturated Fat	2 g
Cholesterol	82 mg
Sodium	167 mg
Carbohydrate	36 g
Dietary Fiber	0 g
Protein	8 g
Calcium	162 mg
Iron	1 mg
Vitamin A	220 RE
Vitamin C	2 mg

DIETARY EXCHANGES:
2 Starch/Bread, ½ Milk,
1 Fat

3 cups water
3 tablespoons honey
1 cup instant nonfat dry milk
2 tablespoons cornstarch
⅛ teaspoon ground cloves
¼ teaspoon ground cinnamon
⅛ teaspoon salt
½ cup cholesterol free egg substitute
½ cup espresso coffee
2 tablespoons orange extract
12 ladyfingers, cut in half lengthwise
¼ cup grated semisweet chocolate

1 Bring water and honey to a boil in medium saucepan over high heat. Reduce heat; simmer, uncovered, 20 minutes. Remove from heat.

2 Combine dry milk, cornstarch, cloves, cinnamon and salt in medium bowl. Slowly add milk mixture to honey mixture, stirring until smooth. Bring to a boil, stirring constantly, over medium heat. Remove from heat.

3 Pour egg substitute into small bowl. Add ½ cup hot milk mixture to egg substitute; blend well. Stir egg mixture back into remaining milk mixture in saucepan. Cook over low heat 2 minutes or until thickened. Cool 15 minutes. Combine coffee with orange extract in another small bowl. Set aside.

4 Arrange 6 ladyfingers in 1-quart serving bowl. Drizzle half the coffee mixture over ladyfingers. Spread half the custard over ladyfingers. Sprinkle with half the grated chocolate. Repeat layers; cover and refrigerate 2 hours. Spoon into individual bowls. Garnish with powdered sugar before serving, if desired.
Makes 6 servings

ORANGE-THYME GRANITÀ IN COOKIE CUPS

Granità is a refreshing fat free dessert. Made with fruit juice, it is also a good source of vitamin C.

Nutrients per Serving:

Calories	187
(30% of calories from fat)	
Total Fat	7 g
Saturated Fat	1 g
Cholesterol	0 mg
Sodium	55 mg
Carbohydrate	31 g
Dietary Fiber	1 g
Protein	3 g
Calcium	30 mg
Iron	1 mg
Vitamin A	68 RE
Vitamin C	61 mg

DIETARY EXCHANGES:
1 Starch/Bread, 1 Fruit,
1 Fat

2½ cups fresh orange juice
½ cup lemon juice
¼ cup sugar
1 teaspoon finely chopped fresh thyme
6 Lemon Anise Cookie Cups (recipe follows)

1 Combine juices, sugar and thyme in medium bowl; stir until sugar dissolves. Freeze until slightly firm, about 1 hour. Beat with wire whisk to break ice crystals. Repeat freezing and beating process 2 to 3 times until ice is firm and granular.

2 To serve, scoop ½ cup granità into each cookie cup. Garnish as desired.

Makes 6 servings

LEMON ANISE COOKIE CUPS

3 tablespoons all-purpose flour
3 tablespoons sugar
2 tablespoons margarine, melted
1 teaspoon grated lemon peel
¼ teaspoon anise extract
1 egg white
¼ cup sliced almonds

1 Preheat oven to 375°F. Combine flour, sugar, margarine, lemon peel, anise extract and egg white in food processor; process until smooth.

2 Spray outside bottoms of 6 custard cups and 2 baking sheets with nonstick cooking spray. Spread 1 tablespoon batter into 5-inch-diameter circle on baking sheet with rubber spatula. Repeat to make total of 6 circles. Sprinkle 2 teaspoons almonds in center of each.

3 Bake 3 to 4 minutes or until edges are browned. Place each cookie over bottom of prepared custard cup so almonds face inside. Press cookies against custard cup to form cookie cup. Cool.

Makes 6 cups

*Personalized Nutrition Reference for Different Calorie Levels**

Daily Calorie Level	1,600	2,000	2,200	2,800
Total Fat	53 g	65 g	73 g	93 g
% of Calories from Fat	30%	30%	30%	30%
Saturated Fat	18 g	20 g	24 g	31 g
Carbohydrate	240 g	300 g	330 g	420 g
Protein	46 g**	50 g	55 g	70 g
Dietary Fiber	20 g***	25 g	25 g	32 g
Cholesterol	300 mg	300 mg	300 mg	300 mg
Sodium	2,400 mg	2,400 mg	2,400 mg	2,400 mg
Calcium	1,000 mg	1,000 mg	1,000 mg	1,000 mg
Iron	18 mg	18 mg	18 mg	18 mg
Vitamin A	1,000 RE	1,000 RE	1,000 RE	1,000 RE
Vitamin C	60 mg	60 mg	60 mg	60 mg

  * Numbers may be rounded
 ** 46 g is the minimum amount of protein recommended for all
    calorie levels below 1,800.
*** 20 g is the minimum amount of fiber recommended for all calorie
    levels below 2,000.

Note: These calorie levels may not apply to children or adolescents, who have
varying calorie requirements. For specific advice concerning calorie levels,
please consult a registered dietitian, qualified health professional or pediatrician.

VOLUME MEASUREMENTS (dry)

⅛ teaspoon = 0.5 mL
¼ teaspoon = 1 mL
½ teaspoon = 2 mL
¾ teaspoon = 4 mL
1 teaspoon = 5 mL
1 tablespoon = 15 mL
2 tablespoons = 30 mL
¼ cup = 60 mL
⅓ cup = 75 mL
½ cup = 125 mL
⅔ cup = 150 mL
¾ cup = 175 mL
1 cup = 250 mL
2 cups = 1 pint = 500 mL
3 cups = 750 mL
4 cups = 1 quart = 1 L

VOLUME MEASUREMENTS (fluid)

1 fluid ounce (2 tablespoons) = 30 mL
4 fluid ounces (½ cup) = 125 mL
8 fluid ounces (1 cup) = 250 mL
12 fluid ounces (1½ cups) = 375 mL
16 fluid ounces (2 cups) = 500 mL

WEIGHTS (mass)

½ ounce = 15 g
1 ounce = 30 g
3 ounces = 90 g
4 ounces = 120 g
8 ounces = 225 g
10 ounces = 285 g
12 ounces = 360 g
16 ounces = 1 pound = 450 g

DIMENSIONS

1/16 inch = 2 mm
⅛ inch = 3 mm
¼ inch = 6 mm
½ inch = 1.5 cm
¾ inch = 2 cm
1 inch = 2.5 cm

OVEN TEMPERATURES

250°F = 120°C
275°F = 140°C
300°F = 150°C
325°F = 160°C
350°F = 180°C
375°F = 190°C
400°F = 200°C
425°F = 220°C
450°F = 230°C

BAKING PAN SIZES

Utensil	Size in Inches/Quarts	Metric Volume	Size in Centimeters
Baking or	8×8×2	2 L	20×20×5
Cake Pan	9×9×2	2.5 L	22×22×5
(square or	12×8×2	3 L	30×20×5
rectangular)	13×9×2	3.5 L	33×23×5
Loaf Pan	8×4×3	1.5 L	20×10×7
	9×5×3	2 L	23×13×7
Round Layer	8×1½	1.2 L	20×4
Cake Pan	9×1½	1.5 L	23×4
Pie Plate	8×1¼	750 mL	20×3
	9×1¼	1 L	23×3
Baking Dish	1 quart	1 L	—
or Casserole	1½ quart	1.5 L	—
	2 quart	2 L	—